Divine Love Letters
Islamic Poetry & Prose

Asyiqin Al-Shaeir

Cetakan Pertama: OKTOBER 2021

Perpustakaan Negara
Malaysia

Cataloguing-in-Publication
Data

Asyiqin al-Shaeir, 1991-
Divine Love Letter : Islamic
Poetry and Poems /
Asyiqin al-Shaeir. ISBN
978-967-26122-0-9

1.Islamic poetry, English.

2. English poetry.

3. English prose literature.

4. Islamic literature.

I.Title. 821.92

HAK CIPTA TERPELIHARA

JAMINAN KUALITI

Sekiranya terdapat masalah dari segi cetakan, sila kembalikan kepada
peruncit dalam tempoh sebulan dari tarikh pembelian untuk digantikan
dengan naskah yang baru. Sebarang pertanyaan boleh hubungi
langsung ke penulis.

Praise for Divine Love Letters

'Divine Love Letters is a complete spiritually awakening journey. It brings you closer to your Lord if someone understands its true essence. A must-read for anyone who finds themselves in the dark and waiting for the light of Lord.'

FAREED SAIFEE

'I don't have words to describe how wonderful Divine Love Letters is. Literally, I got goosebumps. Great work.'

NISAR HUSSEIN

CONTENTS

Acknowledgements

This collection of poetry and prose will not come into being if not for the following people — my good friend, Rakika Rafi, thank you for convincing me to make this book. To all my siblings, you have helped me in your own way, and I could not thank you enough. To my parents, the most special people in my life, only God knows how much I love both of you.

"The Quran is not just a book of guidance.
Allah SWT wrote us a 632 page love letter"
- Anonymous.

Introduction

No one can really explain what moves them to take up a pen and start writing. It is either a journal, short stories or even love letters meant to be sent to someone but stays in the draft document forever, hidden from the world. There is something about writing. You pour out your thoughts on the piece of paper, knowing that this is your own personal space. Through writing, it is as though you are in your own universe—free to create whatever you want in this little universe of yours. You can make it as beautiful and perfect as you wish, or you can create your little universe of darkness full of mysteries.

Each writer has their own fantasies, which reflects through their work. This is our safe space, where we can write up our characters to life. When I first started writing, it was a rather peculiar beginning. I was going through an especially hard time in my life, and I found that the situation that I was in was hard to talk about with anyone. It was then that I realized I have that one friend who understands me. Every time it felt heavy to carry on, I will get out a piece of paper and write to God. Yes, you read it just right. Like a miracle, what was heavy feels light once again.

From letters pouring out my heart to God, my form of writing slowly changed to poetry. I find myself writing poetry a lot, mostly inspired by spiritual topics. Whenever the ideas strike, I will write it down quickly, for surely, I will not remember it again if I did not. However, my fondness towards poetry is not something new. I grew up a big fan of Jalalad-Din Muhammad Rumi, best known worldwide as Rumi. Rumi is the world most famous poet, and I find that his poems always get to me as if it is purely written with the intention to teach. To be able to write spiritual poetry too is an honour.

My poetry is my letter to you. What I have written for you have their own meaning, as the readers will only understand up to the standards of their own knowledge. Some will see it as wise sayings. A few will understand the true meaning. If you are lucky, you will be among the few. Isn't that the dream? To be in a group of people that understands the life and the meaning behind it. As Ibn Arabi says, "All that is left to us by tradition is mere words. It is up to us to find out what they mean." Read, with the eye of your heart. Then there is no veil between you and the truth.

With love,

Asyiqin Al-Shaeir.

For You,
Only You could have made this possible for me.

"All that is left to us by tradition is mere words. It is up to us to understand what they mean "

-Ibn Arabi

"I breathed into you My spirit."

You promised me You will be near,

I looked for You all over,

Years go by and I decided to look within, And I see
You, smiling back at me,

Your promise is true all along,

You are always with me,

Closer to me than my jugular vein.

لقد وعدتني بأنك ستكون قريبا،

بحثت عنك في كل مكان،

مرت سنوات وقررت أن أنظر إلى الداخل، وأنا أراك، وأبتسم لي،

إن وعدك صحيح طوال الوقت،

أنت دائمًا معي،

أقرب إلي من الوريد الوجودي.

Jannah

United as one,
I am so happy,
Everyday feels like
a *paradise* with You.

متحدون كواحد،
أنا سعيد جدا،
كل يوم يشعر بالفردوس معك.

The Art of Awakening

There is a treasure buried deep in your heart,
Waiting patiently to be unearthed by you, Only
when your heart is pure and true,
Will it unveil itself to you.

The light is your map to the *truth,*
Without it, you are like a blind,
Struggling to find the straight path,
The path of the pure and true.

The light itself is a rare gem,
It only reveals itself to the worthy miners,
So rare that only a few have found them,
It will not befriend the heart of sinners.

Once the light enters you,
The straight path unveils itself,
Then you can finally see the *truth,*
And the guardian of the treasure now is you.

فن اليقظة

هناك كنز مدفون في أعماق قلبك،
منتظرين بصبر أن تستخرجي منك،
فقط عندما يكون قلبك نقي وحقيقي،
هل سيكشف عن نفسه لك.

النور هو خريطتك للحق،
بدونه، أنت كالأعمى،
تناضل للعثور على الطريق المستقيم،
سبيل الغني والحق.

الضوء نفسه جوهرة نادرة،
إنها تكشف فقط عن نفسها لعمال المناجم المستحقين،
نادر جدا لدرجة أن القليل فقط قد وجدها،
ولن يصادق قلب الخطاة.

بمجرد دخول الضوء إليك،
المسار المستقيم يكشف عن نفسه،
ثم يمكنك أخيرا رؤية الحقيقة،
و حارس الكنز الآن هو أنت.

Aura

My love,

Do you know the value you behold in My Eyes?

You shine as beautiful as the diamond and as bright
as the sun.

Upon you, I bestowed this enchanting beauty,

That will surely capture any heart,

Simply because you, has captured Mine.

أورا

،حبيبتي

هل تعرف القيمة التي تراها في عيني؟

.تشع بجمال الماسة وبسطوع الشمس

،لقد وهبت لك هذا الجمال الساحر
،هذا بالتأكيد سيخطف أي قلب
.ببساطة لأنك، قد حصلت على بلدي

Mercy

If you want His mercy,

Be merciful toward others,

For you were once in a pit of darkness,

But by His mercy, you have found the light.

رحمة

،إن أردت رحمته

،كن رحيما بالآخرين

،لأنك كنت ذات يوم في حفرة من الظلام

.ولكن برحمته وجدتم النور

HomeSick

They say I am lucky,
They say I am blessed,
Remembering *memories*,
From a world away.
They must not know my agony,
They must not know my pain,
For all I can think about now,
Is that Friend from a world away.

هوم إيبليك

،يقولون أنني محظوظ
،يقولون أنني مباركة
.تذكر الذكريات، من عالم بعيد

،لا يجب أن يعرفوا معاناتي
،لا يجب أن يعرفوا ألمي
،لكل ما يمكنني التفكير به الآن
.هل هذا صديق من عالم بعيد

Faith

Do not be saddened by what they plotted against you.
10 brothers went against Prophet Yusuf,
Yet he was successful.

إيمان

.لا تحزنوا على ما دبروا لكم

أخوة وقعوا على النبي يوسف 10،

.ومع ذلك فقد كان ناجحا

The Art of Living

There will be a time when people are with you,

And there will be a time when people are against you.

Hold on to Him during both times.

فن العيش

سيكون هناك وقت يكون فيه الناس معك،

وسيكون هناك وقت يكون الناس ضدك فيه.

تمسك به في كلا الأزمتين.

Be Wise

Do not love too much,
The one you look up to,
Might be the one
Trying to bring you
down.

Do not hate too much,
The one you dislike
Might be the one
Praying for you
When you are down.

كن حكيما

لا تحبوا كثيرا،
الشخص الذي تبحث عنه،
قد يكون الواحد
محاولة إسقاطك.

لا تكره كثيرا،
الذي تكرهه
قد يكون هو
تصلي لأجلك
لما بتكون جالس.

"Do you remember the promise you have made to Me?"

There are two best friends who are always together, They complete each other like no other, After years of being together, They made a pact to depart from each other, Only to cross path again with each other, For what is *one* can never run away from the other.

" هل تتذكر الوعد الذي قطعته علي؟"

،هناك صديقان مقربان دائمًا معا

،لا يكملون بعضهم البعض

،بعد سنوات من العمل معا

،لقد عقدوا إتفاقا للخروج من بعضهم البعض

،فقط لتعبر المسار مرة أخرى مع بعضها البعض

.فما هو أحد لا يستطيع الهروب من الآخر

Complete Dependence

You are my sun,

I'm merely your moon,

I don't have the light of my
own,

My light is only from You,

With Your love,

I shine brighter than the sun!

تبعية كاملة

انت شمسی؛

أنا مجرد قمرك،

ليس لدي ضوء خاص بي

نوري منك فقط،

مع حبك

أشرق أكثر من الشمس!

The Power of Prayer

No matter what happens,
Never be in despair,
For the help of God,
Is always a prayer away.

قوة الصلاة

،مهما حدث
،لا تيأس أبدا
،من أجل مساعدة الله
.هو دائمًا صلاة

Source of Light

I know you are tired.

Sometimes you don't know who to trust.

One thing is for sure, put your trust in Allah SWT.

He will show you who to trust and who had broken
your trust.

مصدر الضوء

.أعلم أنك متعب

.أحيانا لا تعرف من تثق به

.شي واحد اكيد حطو ثقتكم بالله سبحانه وتعالى

.سيظهر لك من تثق ومن كسر ثقتك

Divine Monologue I

Ya Rabb, why am I always in pain?
"Because I want you to always be in the state of
remembering Me."

Ya Rabb, why does the test never end?
"As long as you breathe, you will
be tested by Me."

Ya Rabb, what is the reason for this trial?
"For you have promised Me, you will conquer all the
tests and come back to Me."

المونولوجات الإلهية الأولى

يا رب، لماذا أنا دائمًا في ألم؟
".لأنني أريدك أن تكون دائمًا في حالة تذكري"

يا رب، لماذا لا ينتهي الاختبار؟
طالما أنك تتنفس، فإنك ستفعل"
.كن تحت إمتحاني

يا رب شو سبب هالمحاكمة ؟
".لأنك وعدتني، ستتغلب على كل الاختبارات وتعود إلى"

Forbearance

Our life is like a rose,

A lot of thorns are thrown in our paths,
But if we are patient enough,

There it is in all its glory,

Full bloom of *roses*, waiting for us.

صبر

،حياتنا مثل الورد

،كثير من الأشواك ترمى في طرقنا

،ولكن إذا كنا صبورين بما فيه الكفاية

،ها هي في كل مجدها

.زهرة الورد كاملة، في انتظارنا

Mercy

Never give up on the mercy of your Lord,

No matter how dark your past is,

Always run back to Him,

You will find Him there,

Smiling at You and say,

"I am glad you found your way back to Me."

رحمة

،لا تقلع عن رحمة ربك أبدا

،مهما كان ماضيك مظلما

،دائمًا أرتد إليه

،ستجده هناك

،تبتسم لك وتقول

"أنا سعيد لأنك وجدت طريق العودة إلى".

Knowledge

Do not be sad if they can't see things the way you do,

You cannot force the blind to see,

The deaf to hear,

And the mute to speak.

معرفة

لا تحزن إذا لم يكن بمقدورهم رؤية الأمور بالطريقة التي تريدها،

لا يمكنك فرض الأعمى يرى،

الصم الذين يسمعونهم،

والبكم الذي يتكلم.

Traveller

My whole life,

I have been a traveler,

Trying to find my way back home,
Carefully, I orchestrate my moves,

For one wrong turn, could cost me *home*.

مسافرة

،طوال حياتي

،لقد كنت مسافرا

،أحاول إيجاد طريقي إلى الوطن

،بحذر، أنا أنسق حركتي

.ولمجرد منعطف خاطئ واحد، يمكن ان يكلفني البيت

Jealousy

Jealousy is the root of all evil,
It turned the leader of
angels,
Into the leader of hell.

غيرة

الغيرة أصل كل الشرور؛
لقد أصبح قائد الملائكة
إلى قائد الجحيم

Justice

Never be like the stepbrothers of *Yusuf* A.S,

Trying to destroy your own blood,

Out of sheer jealousy,

For your evil plans might succeed,

But be afraid cause it is He who is going to stand up,

For the *Yusuf* of the world,

And take them out of the well,

To the *noble* position,

where they belong.

عدالة

،لا تكن أبدا مثل إخوة يوسف أ.س

،محاولة تدمير دمك

،بدافع الغيرة المطلقة

،لأن خططك الشريرة قد تنجح

بس خاف لأنو هو يلي بدو يقوم

،من أجل يوسف العالم

،وإخراجهم من البئر

،إلى الموقف النبيل

.حيث ينتمون

The Game of Life

Carefully planning their move, With all seriousness,
In the game of chess.

Knowing very well, That one wrong move,

Can throw them off the game.

If only you plan this life like you treat,

The game of chess.

Not making reckless moves,

That will make you lose,

And fall to the gate of hell.

لعبة الحياة

ويخططون بعناية لتحركاتهم بكل جدية،
في لعبة الشطرنج.

مع العلم جيدا، تلك خطوة خاطئة،
يمكن أن يرميها من اللعبة.

لو فقط خططت لهذه الحياة كما تتعامل
لعبة الشطرنج.

لا تقوم بخطوات متهورة،
هذا سيجعلك تخسر،
وسقط إلى باب الهاوية.

Declaration of War

Beware of who you hurt,
For they might be a friend of God,
For whenever they are hurt,
There is a wrath of God.

اعلان الحرب

إحذر من تؤذي،
لأنهم قد يكونون أصدقاء لله،
كلما تأذى،
هناك غضب من الله.

Beware

God's mercy overcomes His wrath,

But do not let it make you careless,

He is also The Most Just,

So do repent before you are breathless.

احترس

،رحمة الله تتغلب على غضبه

،ولكن لا تدعه يجعلك مهملا

،وهو أيضا الأكثر عدلا

.هكذا توبوا قبل ان تكونوا بلا نفس

Long Lost Friend

Do not be afraid,

To lose friends and lovers,
For through these losses,
You might gain,

Your true *Friend* back.

صديق مفقود منذ زمن طويل

لا تخف،

لفقدان أصدقاء وعشاق،

عن طريق هذه الخسائر،

قد تكسب،

صديقك القديم.

Sealed

The secret is out in the open,
It wants to be known,
But it is the hardest to open,
Only a few have known.

ختم

،السر في العراء
،يريد أن يعرف
،ولكن من الصعب فتحها
.ولم يعرف إلا القليل

True Healing

Everyone wants to heal,
But if your sickness,
Brings you closer to
Him,
You are indeed *healed*.

شفاء حقيقي

،الجميع يريد الشفاء
لكن إذا مرضك
يقربك منه أكثر
.قد شفيت

Surrender

Some fate are written with a pen while some are
written with a pencil.

May you have the strength to accept what you cannot
change and be humble to bow down and beg for a
better fate.

إستسلام

.ويكتب قدر ما بقلم بينما يكتب بعضها بقلم رصاص

وليكن لديكم القوة لتقبلوا ما لا يمكنكم تغييره
.ولتتواضعوا لتسجدوا وتطلبوا مصيرا افضل

Karamat

If you only knew how dangerous it is to set traps for
friends of God,

You might try to prevent them from reaching for the
stars,

But He will stand up for them,

And gifted them the
moon.

كرامات

،إذا كنت تعرف فقط مدى خطورة وضع الفخاخ لصديق الله

،قد تحاول منعهم من الوصول إلى النجوم، فيدافع عنهم

.و نعطيهم القمر

Slander

Never simply believe any rumours that you hear,

For you might be hearing from Abdullah,

In his attempt to slander Aisyah R.A.

إغتيابا

،لا تصدق أبدا ببساطة أي شائعات تسمعها

،لعلكم تسمعون من عبدالله

في محاولته التشهير بعائشة آر. أي

Forbidden fruit

The haram is like a forbidden fruit,
As tempting as it is,
Taking a bite of it is a sin,
From heaven you will fall,
Regretting you ever took a bite at all.

فاكهة محظورة

،الحرام مثل الفاكهة المحرمة، بقدر ما هو مغري
،تناول لدغة منها خطيئة
،من الجنة
،ستسقط
.ندم على أنك أخذت قضمة على الإطلاق

Divine Intervention

If there is a Yaajuj and Maajuj in your life,
Do not be afraid,
He will definitely send,
A *Dzulkarnain* your way.

التدخل الإلهي

إذا كان في حياتكن يعوج ومعجوج،
لا تخف،
سيرسل بالتأكيد،
أ. زولكارنين بطريقتك.

Repentance

No matter how pious you are,
Never look down on others,
For today's sinner,
Might be tomorrow's saint.

توبة

بغض النظر عن مدى تقوتك،
لا تحتقروا الآخرين
بالنسبة للخاطئ اليوم،
ربما يكون قديس الغد

Muhammad

When there is an Abu Jahal among you,
Do not be sad,
For there is a Muhammad in you,
That will take a stand.

محمد

، لما يكون فيك أبو جهل
،لا تحزن
،لأنه فيك محمد
.هذا سيأخذ موقفا

Betrayal never comes from stranger

Be careful in trusting others,

Even Qabil,

Killed Habil.

الخيانه عمرها ما بتجي من الغريب

،كن حذرا في الثقة بالآخرين

،حتى قابيل

.قتلت هابيل

Crossroad

This life is like the *golden calf*,

It was entrusted to you by the One,
Protect it or destroy it,

Is the ultimate test,

Only a Few will pass it,

While the rest will burn in hell.

تقاطع الطرق

هذه الحياة مثل العجل الذهبي،

لقد عهد إليك من قبل الواحد،

حمايته أو تدميره،

هو الاختبار النهائي

قليلون فقط سينجحون

والباقي سيحترق في الجحيم.

Gains and Losses

They blame it all on fate,

If that is true,

Why did He created the heaven and the
hell?

المكاسب والخسائر

فهم يلومون كل شيء على القدر،

إذا كان ذلك صحيحا،

لماذا خلق السماء والجحيم؟

Awliya

The friends of God, Is under His dome,
Identity locked, Safe and secured.

Go about this world with care,
Because those that you hurt might be the friend,
Of the Lord of the world.

أوليا

،أصدقاء الله، تحت قبته
.الهوية مؤمنة وآمنة ومأمونة

،اذهبوا حول هذا العالم بعناية
،لأن تلك التي تؤذيها قد تكون صديقة
.من رب العالمين

Choices

My love,

No matter how far you may
wander,

You will come back to Me,

That is not up for you to choose.
But,

My love,

To come back to Me with honor,
Or to come back to Me in disgrace,

That is up to you to choose.

الخيارات

حبيبتي،
بغض النظر عن المسافة التي تقطعها،
ستعود إلى،
هذا ليس من إختيارك.

ولكن،

حبيبتي،
أن أعود إلى بشرف،
أو أن أعود إلى بخزي،
وهذا يرجع إليك في الاختيار.

Divine Monologue II

Ya Rab, there is this feeling of deep sadness in me.

"Talk to Me, I will respond to you."

I'm sad over my yearning for this world.

"I created humans to have many needs.

Whether you master your lust

For the sake of Me.

Or you let it mastered you,
For the sake of this world
That is the test,

That you need to pass,
For the sake of Me."

المونولوجات الإلهية الثانية

يا رب في فيي إحساس عميق بالحزن.
"تحدثي معي، سأرد عليك".
أنا حزين على اشتياقي لهذا العالم.

"لقد خلقت بشرا لديهم إحتياجات كثيرة. سواء كنت تتقن شهوتك
من أجلي.
أو تتركيه يتفوق عليك، لأجل هذا العالم الذي هو الاختبار،
يجب أن تمر، من أجلي.

Iman

It is okay to fall,
But still bow down to God.
Instead of flying high,
but bow down not to the One.

إيمان

،لا بأس من السقوط
.ولكن مع ذلك سجدوا لله
.عوضا عن الطيران عاليا ولكن ليس إلى أسفل

The Candle

Do not be sad,
If you are in the dark,
For only in darkness,
Can you see the *light*.

الشمعة

،لا تحزن
،إذا كنت في الظلام
،فقط في الظلام
.هل يمكنك رؤية الضوء

Perseverance

Have faith!

For that is all that you need in this world,

Your faith is what between you and Him,
The stronger your faith in Him,

The closer you are to Him,

Hence, the closer you are, To the *truth*.

Do not be weak!

The weakness of the heart will lead you,

To weakness of iman,

That is a bridge between you and satan,
The weaker you are,

The closer you are to satan,

Hence, the farther you are from the *truth*.

مثابرة

كن مؤمنا!
لأن هذا كل ما تحتاجه في هذا العالم،
إيمانك هو ما بينك وبين هيرن،
كلما كان إيمانك في هيرن أقوى،
كلما اقتربت من هيرن،
لذلك كلما اقتربت أكثر من الحق.

لا تكن ضعيفا!
ضعف القلب سيقودك،
إلى ضعف إرنان،
هذا جسر بينك وبين الشيطان،
كلما كنت أضعف،
كلما اقتربت من الشيطان،
لذلك كلما ابتعدت عن الحق.

Tauhid

A believer will believe in God,
Even when leading the most ordinary life.

A disbeliever will not believe in God,
Even if you present them food from the sky.

توهيدي

،المؤمن يؤمن بالله
.حتى عندما تعيش حياة عادية جدا

،الكافر لا يؤمن بالله
.حتى لو قدمتموهم الطعام من السماء

The Real Fortunate

In this life, be like the blind, the deaf, and the mute,

The blind are those who guard their eyes against
sinful things,

The deaf are those who guard their ears against
hearing lies and rumors,

The mute are those who guard their tongue against
backbiting and lying.

المحظوظ الحقيقي

،في هذه الحياة، كن كالأعمى والصم والبكم

،الأعمى هم الذين يحرسون أعينهم من الحرام

،إن الصم هم الذين يحفظون آذانهم من سماع الأكاذيب والشائعات

.البكم هم الذين يحفظون لسانهم من الرجعية والكذب

Priorities

Do not run after this world,

Like it is the hereafter,

Rather you should run from this
world,

And chase the hereafter.

أولويات

لا تركض بعد هذا العالم

كأنها الآخرة

بل يجب أن تهرب من هذا العالم

واتبع الآخرة

Arrogance

Never think you are better than everyone else,

Thinking that alone is making you less than everyone else.

غطرسة

لا تعتقد أنك أفضل من أي شخص آخر

التفكير في ذلك وحده يجعلك أقل من أي شخص آخر

Influences

Do not befriend,

Those who like to spread rumors,

For you consider them a friend while to them,
You are just another rumour.

التأثيرات

لا تصادق

،الذين يحبون نشر الاشاعات

،لأنك تعتبرهم صديقا بينما بالنسبة لهم

.أنت مجرد إشاعة أخرى

Ties of Blood

Never give up on your family,
For they are entrusted to you by the One,
Do not cut ties no matter what,
They might one day repent to the One.

روابط الدم

لا تتخلى عن عائلتك أبدا،
لأنهم ائتمنوا عليك من الواحد،
لا تقطع العلاقات مهما حدث،
فقد يتوبون يوما إلى الواحد.

Soldier

If you found yourself in a battlefield,
Then know that He sees you as a
soldier.

جندي

،إذا وجدت نفسك في ساحة المعركة
إذا، اعرف أنه سيراك كجندي

Between the lines

Secrets are whispered between the lines, saying, "Come back, you have been gone long enough."

سر

تهمس الأسرار بين السطور، قائلة: "عد، لقد مضى
وقت طويل بما فيه الكفاية"

Pillars of Faith

Prayer is a bridge to God,

To use it and cross to the other side,

Or to abandon it and drown,

Will determine the state you are on the other *side*.

أركان الإيمان

،الصلاة جسر إلى الله

،لاستعمالها والعبور إلى الجانب الآخر

،أو أن يهجرها ويغرق

.هتحدد الحاله اللى انت فيها في الناحية التانية

The Calling

Only you know your true calling,
To fulfill it or ignore it,
Is going to decide whether you truly,
Deserve your calling.

الدعوة

أنت فقط تعرف إتصالك الحقيقي،
ولتنفيذ ذلك،
أو تجاهله،
سوف تقرر ما إذا كنت حقا، تستحق دعوتك.

Silver Lining

He is calling to us,
Every second of the time,
Through every heartbreak,
Through every loss,
Through every sickness,
That finally make us stand up,
On the prayer mat and *kneel*.

بطانة فضية

إنه يتصل بنا،
كل ثانية من الوقت،
من خلال كل حسرة شعرنا بها،
من خلال كل خسارة لدينا،
من خلال كل مرض نعانيه،
هذا أخيرا يجعلنا نقف،
على سجادة الصلاة و ركع.

Diamond

Even the ugly charcoal,

Need pressure to become,

A beautiful diamond,

That is the same as you and I.

Do not be sad over the
pressure,

That life has on you,

It is simply to turn you,

Into the jewel you are.

ألماس

حتى الفحم القبيح
تحتاج إلى الضغط لتصير
الماسة الجميلة
هذا هو نفس الشيء الذي أنا وأنت

لا تحزن على الضغط
تلك الحياة عليك
إنه ببساطة أن تتحول إليك
في جوهرة أنت.

Unbeaten

Ifrit claimed he could bring in the throne,

Before Prophet Sulaiman A.S get up from his throne,

The friend of God claimed he could bring in the throne,

Before Prophet Sulaiman A.S blink his eyes,

I hope you understand by this story,

That in the end,

The winner is the One on the throne.

غير مقيد

،وادعى إيفريت أنه يستطيع أن يجلب العرش

،قبل اعتلاء رسول الله صلى الله عليه وسلم عرشه

،ادعى صديق الله أنه يستطيع أن يجلب العرش

،قبل أن يغمض النبي سليمان ع. أعينه

،أرجو أن تستوعبوا هذه القصة

.أن في النهاية الفائز هو من على العرش

God Over All

In making decisions,

Be like Ibrahim A.S,

When torn into two,

Always decide to choose the One.

الله على الجميع

،في إتخاذ القرارات

،كن مثل إبراهيم ق.س

،عندما تمزق إلى نصفين

.قرر دائمًا إختيار واحد

Repentance

This life is like a pure white fabric,

The more sins we make,

The more tainted the white fabric.

But, never think of the stain as permanent,

For we can always wash it clean,

With honest repentance as the detergent.

توبة

،هذه الحياة مثل نسيج أبيض نقي

،كلما إرتكبنا خطايا أكثر

.كلما أفسد النسيج الأبيض أكثر

،ولكن، لا تفكر أبدا في هذا البصمة على أنها دائمة

،لأننا نستطيع دائمًا غسلها نظيفة

.وتوبة صادقة بصفتها الراعية

The Pure

Beware of those,

With the eye of the heart,

For the eye that can see,
Through space and time,
Has no problem,

Seeing your bunch of lies.

الطاهر

،إحذروا منها

،بعين القلب

،للعين التي تستطيع أن ترى

،خلال فترة من الزمن

،لا توجد مشكلة

.رؤية مجموعة الأكاذيب الخاصة بك

Believer

Have a strong faith,

Like the people of the cave,

Any problems that you have,

Have complete trust and faith.

The faith in Him is going to save,

Even in deep sleep, sound and safe,

You wake up the next morning in the *cave*,
Amazed that you are now safe.

مصدقا

لديك إيمان قوي،
مثل أهل الكهف،
أي مشاكل لديك،
امتلكوا ثقة وإيمانا كاملين.

هذا الإيمان به سينقذ،
حتى في حالة النوم العميق، السليم والآمن،
تستيقظ في الصباح التالي في الكهف،
أدهشكم انكم الآن في امان.

Gratitude

Do not be an ungrateful child,

Causing troubles instead of delight,

The wrath of your parents is not light,

It evokes the wrath of God on your life,

So care for them right,

And be a grateful child.

إمتنان

،لا تكن طفلا ناكرا للجميل

،مما يسبب المشاكل بدلا من البهجة

،غضب والديك ليس ضوءا

،إنه يثير غضب الله على حياتك

،لذا اهتم بهم جيدا

.وكن طفلا شاكرا

Parents

Parents are a gift to you,
To accompany you in this world,
Treasure and cherish them with you,
Before they leave for the other world.

آباء

،الآباء هدية لك
،لمرافقتك في هذا العالم
،أعزهم و أعزهم معك
.قبل أن يغادروا إلى العالم الآخر

The Key

This life is a prison,
We are all looking for our way out,
Love for this world is imprisonment,
Love for Him is the only way out.

المفتاح

،هذه الحياة سجن
،نحن جميعا نبحث عن طريقنا للخروج
،حب هذا العالم هو السجن
.فالمحبة له هي المخرج الوحيد

On Repeat

If you go through the same test,

Over and over again,

That means you are failing the same test,

Over and over again.

عند التكرار

إذا مررت بنفس الاختبار،

مرارا وتكرارا،

هذا يعني أنك فشلت في نفس الاختبار،

مرارا وتكرارا.

Secret

The soul knows the secret,

For it is told a long time ago,

It is your job to uncover the *secret,*

By being as pure as you were a long time ago.

سر

،الروح تعرف السر

،لأنه قيل منذ زمن طويل

،وظيفتك هي كشف السر

.بكونك نقي كما كنت منذ زمن طويل

The Teaching

After being a guru for some time, Muhammad is
frustrated by some of his student's inability to
understand what he teaches. Muhammad takes a day
off to go to his guru's house, the one who moulded
him to be the man he is today. "Why do you look
upset, Muhammad?" asked his guru. "I'm concern I'm
not doing it the right way. I found some of my
students still in the beginner level despite spending
years with me." said Muhammad sadly.

"Muhammad, I want you to take a walk with me
to the town." Muhammad is taken aback by his
guru's request but after spending years under his
wings, he has learned not to question any of his guru's
demands. They walk together to the town, where there
are shouts of people trying to sell off their
products—fabrics, sheep, human slaves, you name it.
"Now, Muhammad. I want you to go to that beggar
and teach him colours till he knows every shades of
colours that exists in this world." Muhammad nodded
at his guru and thought to himself, 'How is teaching
such a simple thing to a mere stranger going to solve
my teaching problems?'

Still, he obeyed his guru and walked across the street to the beggar who was sleeping in a seating position, although in front of him is a spread of rugs he has been using for sleeping. "Assalamualaikum!" said Muhammad "Waalaikummussalam" said the beggar, cheerfully. Muhammad was taken aback at how fast the beggar replies and he realised that the beggar wasn't sleeping at all. His eyes are shut because he is blind.

Panicking, Muhammad donated one dinar and walked back across the street to his guru. "Master, you need to choose another man for this teaching lesson as it is impossible for me to teach that particular beggar."

"Why is that so, Muhammad?" asked his guru.

"Because he is blind, Master. You cannot teach the blind any colours at all. It is just impossible." Explained Muhammad. "Indeed, Muhammad. Do you understand now?" Said the guru with a smile.

"Verily, with Every Hardship Comes Ease."

This life is nothing but a test. We are all gifted in a different way. Some with riches, some with strength, some with good looks, and some with wisdom. Like I said, this life is a test. What you are blessed with today might turn against you tomorrow.

We all know of how Prophet Ayub A.S goes from being one of the wealthiest to being poor in a blink of an eye.

We all read of how Prophet Musa A.S was full of remorse, when he accidentally killed someone with a single punch.

We all heard of how Prophet Yusuf A.S's good looks had made him the target of intense jealousy and inappropriate harassment.

We all are aware of how Prophet Adam A.S ate the forbidden fruit despite being taught of wisdom from God Himself.

If you are going through some hard test right now, I hope you will never give up on the help from Allah SWT.

Simply because,

He turned Ayub A.S's situation from being a poor to insanely wealthy again in just a blink of an eye.

He forgave Musa A.S and honored him the ability to speak to Him through a veil.

He saved Yusuf A.S from the torments of his enemies and granted him the noble position that he deserved.

He forgave Adam A.S and reunited him with Hawa even after many years of separation.

Through these stories, I hope you see,

That Allah SWT mercy,

Truly embraces all things.

The Oath

Together we are so happy,

You are my Everything,

You taught me beautiful things.

One day, everything has changed for us.

You decided it was time for us to separate,

I do not understand why but You are The Most Knowing,

I love You so much I took an oath that I will come back to You,

You sealed our stories deep in my heart.

"Only true love towards Me can make you remember our stories," He declared.

"Muhammad, I have taught you all you need to know. Now, you are ready," He said.

"Ready for what, my Lord?" Asked Muhammad

"The biggest trial ya Muhammad. Swear by Me, Muhammad, that you will pass the test?"

"Will You be with me through it all?" He asked.

"Remember Me only then will I remember you," He said.

"I swear by You, my Lord. I will find my way back to the straight path." Muhammad declared his oath. "Only if you pass this test can we be together again forever, Muhammad; please pass this test."
And He sends e off to this new world.

Born as a naive baby,
Crying out loud,
Because the pain of separation ,
Is too much to bear.

Turn the page for a sneak peak at
Asyiqin Al-Shaeir's new book.

A Treasury of Divine Poetry.

The Writing

Muhammad is working on his book. Sometimes he writes at a steady pace. Other times he frown & crumble up the papers. His guru walk in Muhammad's writing place and saw a pile of papers crumbled on the floor. Muhammad is looking rather distressed and is taking a break from today's writing session. "Assalamualaikum ya Muhammad." said the guru. "Waalaikummussalam, guru." answered Muhammad, rather startled by his guru's surprise visit. "I see that you have started your writing journey?" Said the guru, nodding at the pile of papers on the floor.

Muhammad quickly ushers his guru to sit down and pour him a cup of tea. Sitting across his guru, Muhammad sighs. "It is not as easy as I thought it would be." His guru takes a sip of his tea and nodded. "Explain to me what is so hard about it, Muhammad, perhaps I can help." Muhammad explain. "I'm worried that I'm revealing too much in my book. I'm trying my best to tone it down. It is my responsibility to guard the divine secret. How do I write without revealing what is supposed to be hidden?"

His guru chuckled. "Muhammad, have you
forgotten? He revealed all of His secrets in the
open, but did everyone understand?" asked the guru.
"No..." said, Muhammad. The guru smiles
knowingly. "Exactly. The secret is out there in the
obvious but why can't most people know about it,
Muhammad?" asked him again. "It is because of the
veil in their heart." Answered Muhammad quietly,
almost like whispering. "That's the answer to your
question, Muhammad." Said his guru, putting down
his cup of tea.

"Write all you want. Only the one who reads with
the eye of the heart will understand what you are
trying deliver. And why is that, Muhammad?"
Asked
his guru, testing him. "For there is no veil between
them and the truth." Answered Muhammad,
smiling.

Follow Asyiqin Al-Shaeir Official Instagram

@asyiqin_al_shaeir

Scan QR Code